Heartwood

by Knit Picks

Printed in the United States of America

First Printing, 2014

ISBN 978-1-62767-056-2

Versa Press, Inc
800-447-7829

www.versapress.com

CONTENTS

CABLE MESH PULLOVER

by Kerin Dimeler-Laurence

FINISHED MEASUREMENTS

32 (36, 40, 44, 48, 52, 56, 60, 64)" finished bust measurement

YARN

Knit Picks *Palette* (100% Peruvian Highland Wool; 231 yards/50g): Shoal 26054, 6 (7, 8, 9, 10, 11, 12, 13, 14) balls.

NEEDLES

US 3 (3.25mm) DPNs and 24-48" circular needles, or long circulars for Magic Loop, or size to obtain gauge

US 2 (2.75 mm) DPNs and 24-48" circular needles, or one size smaller than gauge needles, for ribbing

NOTIONS

Tapestry Needle
Stitch markers
Scrap yarn or stitch holders
Cable Needle

GAUGE

28 sts and 38 rows = 4" in eyelet pattern, blocked.

Cable Mesh Pullover

Notes:

The paneled pullover gets a lacy update in this lightweight pullover. Even the cable panels have lace. The sleeves are knit in the round from the cuff up to the sleeve cap where it is knit flat. The pullover body is knit from the hem up in the round to the armholes. All references to *Right* and *Left* are as worn, unless otherwise noted.

Three-needle Bind Off

Hold the two pieces of knitting together with the points of the needles facing to the right. Insert a third needle into the first stitch on each of the needles knitwise, starting with the front needle. Work a knit stitch, pulling the loop through both of the stitches you've inserted the third needle through. After you've pulled the loop through, slip the first stitch off of each of the needles. This takes two stitches (one from the front needle and one from the back) and joins them to make one finished stitch on the third needle (held in your right hand). Repeat this motion, inserting your needle into one stitch on the front and back needles, knitting them together and slipping them off of the needles. Each time you complete a second stitch, pass the first finished stitch over the second and off of the needle (as you would in a traditional bind-off).

DIRECTIONS
Sleeves (Make 2)

The sleeves begin in the round at the wrist and are increased to the underarm. They are then worked flat through the sleeve cap.

With smaller needles, CO 72 (76, 80, 84, 88, 92, 96, 100, 100) sts. Join to work in the round, being careful not to twist sts. Work in K1, P1 rib for 2". Switch to larger needles and start working the Sleeve pattern.

Sleeve Pattern

Setup Rnd: K 16 (18, 20, 22, 24, 26, 28, 30, 30), PM, p2, k6, p2, k20, p2, k6, p2, PM, k to end of rnd.

Rnd 2: Work row 2 of Sleeve Border Right, SM, work row 2 of Sleeve Center, SM, work row 2 of Sleeve Border Left.

Work 10 more rnds in pattern, continuing to work from the charts. The 4 rounds of the Border charts and the 12 rounds of the Sleeve Center chart are repeated for the length of the sleeve and sleeve cap.

Sleeve Increases

Note: As you increase, the repeats of the Border charts will change. Keep existing sts in established pattern, only introducing a new YO/decrease repeat when you have sufficient stitches; until then, work any extra stitches near the increases as St st. (e.g.: if round 4 of the chart is an increase row for you, knit the first stitch and increase instead of working the first K2tog/YO pair. Knit the stitch that would be a YO in the chart, then continue working from stitch 3 in the chart.)

Increase Round: K1, M1L, work in pattern to last st, M1R, K1. 2 sts increased.

Continuing in pattern as established, work an Increase Round

every 17th (15th, 13th, 11th, 7th, 5th, 4th , 4th, [4th and 3rd]) round 8 (9, 11, 13, 20, 28, 32, 33, 17) times. 88 (94, 102, 110, 128, 148, 160, 166, 172) sts

Work 14 (13, 5, 15, 14, 14, 12, 0, 1) rounds in pattern, ending on an odd-numbered row.

Sleeve Cap Shaping

The sleeve cap should begin on what will be a WS (even-numbered on the chart) row. On the next round, stitches are bound off at the base of the sleeve cap. The cap is then worked flat (back and forth) to the end.

Work to 5 (5, 4, 4, 4, 4, 5, 4, 5) sts before the end of the round. BO the last 5 (5, 4, 4, 4, 4, 5, 4, 5) sts of the round, then the first 7 (7, 6, 6, 6, 6, 7, 6, 7) sts of the next round. Work in pattern to the last 3 sts of the row, SSSK. You are now working flat over 74 (80, 90, 98, 116, 136, 146, 154, 158) sts.

Double Decrease Row (2 sts decreased at each edge):
RS: K3tog , work in pattern to last 3 sts, SSSK.
WS: P3tog TBL, work in pattern to last 3 sts, P3tog.

Single Decrease Row (1 st decreased at each edge):
RS: K2tog , work in pattern to last 2 sts, SSK.
WS: P2tog TBL, work in pattern to last 2 sts, P2tog.

Continuing in pattern, work a Double Decrease Row every row 0 (1, 1, 2, 2, 3, 3, 4, 4) times;
work a Single Decrease Row every row 3 (4, 4, 4, 7, 10, 13, 11, 11) times, then
every other row 5 (5, 5, 6, 7, 11, 13, 13, 11) times, then
every third row 7 (7, 10, 11, 8, 5, 9, 10, 13) times, then
every other row 5 (5, 5, 5, 7, 7, 4, 7, 12) times, then
every row 4 (4, 4, 4, 8, 6, 6, 5, 5)4 (4, 5, 5, 10, 5, 6, 6, 8) times;
work a Double Decrease Row every row 1 (1, 2, 2, 3, 6, 6, 6, 4) times.

BO the 22 remaining sts.

Body

The body begins with the same ribbing as the sleeves.

With smaller needles, CO 224 (252, 280, 308, 336, 364, 392, 420, 448) sts. PM and join to work in the round, being careful not to twist sts.

Work in K1, P1 rib for 2" or desired depth; place a marker after 112 (126, 140, 154, 168, 182, 196, 210, 224) sts to mark right underarm. Switch to larger needles.

Start working from the Body pattern chart, following repeats as given with the chart. The Body pattern consists of a center mesh panel flanked by cable panels and then side mesh panels.

Set-up Rnd: *K 1(2, 1, 2, 1, 2, 1, 2, 1), PM, K 16 (20, 28, 34, 40, 42, 48, 54, 62) – side mesh panel, P2, K6, P2 – 10-st cable panel, K 58 (62, 62, 62, 66, 74, 78, 78, 78) – center mesh panel, P2, K6, P2 – 10-st cable panel, K 16 (20, 28, 34, 40, 42, 48, 54, 62) – side mesh panel, PM, K 1(2, 1, 2, 1, 2, 1, 2, 1), rep from * once more.

Rnd 2: *K to marker, SM, work from row 2 of Body pattern chart, following repeats as given with the chart, SM, K to marker, rep from * once more.

Work body in pattern, repeating the 12 rows of the chart, until body measures 15.5 (15.5, 15.75, 16, 16.25, 16.25, 16.25, 16, 16)" from cast on, or desired length; ending on an even-numbered round.

Armholes

Note: The armholes are worked over the diagonal lace panels that run to the sides of the cable motifs. A selvedge stitch should remain at the edge of the armscyes. Keep existing sts in established pattern, only working a YO/decrease repeat when you have sufficient stitches, excluding the selvedge stitch and the number of stitches required to complete any decreases. (*e.g.,* if working an Armhole Double Decrease Row, work as many YO/decrease pairs as can fit with 4 sts remaining at the armhole edge; 3 for the decrease, and one selvedge stitch at the edge.) Work any sts that don't fit within a YO/decrease pair as St st. On the next round (an odd-numbered rnd), stitches are bound off at each armhole. After this, the Front and Back are worked flat separately to the shoulders. All armhole decreases take place over the Mesh stitch sections.

Work in pattern to 6 (5, 5, 7, 9, 9, 10, 10, 16) sts before the right underarm marker. BO the next 12 (10, 10, 14, 18, 18, 20, 20, 32) sts, removing marker. Work in pattern to 6 (5, 5, 7, 9, 9, 10, 10, 16) sts before the left underarm marker, BO the last 6 (5, 5, 7, 9, 9, 10, 10, 16) sts of the round and the first to 6 (5, 5, 7, 9, 9, 10, 10, 16) sts of the next round, removing marker.

100 (114, 130, 140, 150, 164, 176, 190, 192) sts remain across both Front and Back. Place Back sts on scrap yarn or a stitch holder.

Front

Shape Armholes

Armhole Double Decrease Row (2 sts decreased each side):
RS: K3tog, work in pattern to last 3 sts, SSSK.
WS: P3tog TBL, work in pattern to last 3 sts, P3tog.

Armhole Single Decrease Row (1 st decreased each side):
RS: K2tog, work in pattern to last 2 sts, SSK.
WS: P2tog TBL, work in pattern to last 2 sts, P2tog.

** Work in pattern (RS on an even-numbered row) across Front. Then work armhole decreases starting on the next (WS) row:

Work an Armhole Double Decrease Row every row 0 (1, 1, 2, 3, 3, 3, 5, 5) times.
Work an Armhole Single Decrease Row every row 3 (2, 2, 3, 4, 4, 6, 6, 7) times.
[Work 4 (2, 2, 2, 2, 2, 2, 2, 2) rows even and then Single Decrease Row once] 1 (1, 2, 3, 2, 2, 2, 2, 2) times.
[Work 6 (3, 3, 3, 3, 3, 3, 3, 3) rows even and then Single Decrease Row once] 1 (1, 1, 1, 2, 2, 1, 2, 2) times.
[Work 4 rows even and then Single Decrease Row once] 0 (1, 1, 1, 1, 1, 1, 0, 0] times. 84 (92, 104, 106, 110, 124, 130, 134, 134) sts **Work 14 (11, 18, 20, 21, 25, 25, 28, 34) rows in pattern, ending with a WS row.

Neckline

On the next RS row, sts are bound off at the front neck to form the neckline. Work these decreases as for the armholes, keeping the edge sts in St st and working only complete sets of YO/decrease pairs.

Work in pattern across the first 36 (39, 45, 46, 48, 54, 57, 59, 59) sts, BO the next 12 (14, 14, 14, 14, 16, 16, 16, 16) sts; work in pattern to end. Follow neckline decrease directions below; attach a second ball of yarn at the left neckline edge and work both sides of the neckline together.

Neckline Double Decrease Row:

RS: Work in pattern to last 3 sts of left neck edge, SSSK. K3tog, work in pattern across right shoulder.
WS: Work in pattern to last 3 sts of right neck edge, P3tog. P3tog TBL, work in pattern across left shoulder.

Neckline Single Decrease Row:

RS: Work in pattern to last 2 sts of left neck edge, SSK. K2tog, work in pattern across right shoulder.
WS: Work in pattern to last 2 sts of right neck edge, P2tog. P2tog TBL, work in pattern across left shoulder.

Shape Neckline:

Work a Neckline Double Decrease Row every row 3 (4, 5, 4, 4, 4, 5, 5, 5) times; work a Neckline Single Decrease Row every row 7 (5, 6, 7, 8, 9, 8, 8, 8) times, then every other row 7 (6, 7, 9, 10, 8, 8, 7, 7) times, then every third row 0 (3, 0, 0, 0, 2, 2, 2, 2) times, then every fourth row 1 (0, 1, 1, 0, 2, 2, 2, 2) times. Work 15 (16, 16, 12, 13, 2, 2, 4, 4) rows in pattern.

21 (23, 24, 25, 26, 29, 30, 29, 29) sts have been removed from each front; 15 (16, 21, 21, 22, 25, 27, 30, 30) sts remain on each shoulder.

Short rows

A set of short rows finishes off the shoulders. Work Left and Right shoulders separately.

Right Shoulder

Short Row 1 (RS): Work in pattern to 4 (5, 6, 6, 7, 8, 8, 10, 10) sts before the; W&T.
Short Row 2 (WS): Work in pattern to end.
Short Row 3: Work in pattern to 4 (5, 6, 6, 7, 8, 8, 10, 10) sts before the wrapped st, W&T.
Short Row 4: Work in pattern to end.
Next Row: Work in pattern across all sts, picking up wrapped sts and knitting them together with the sts they wrap.

Left Shoulder

Short Row 1 (RS): Work in pattern to end.
Short Row 2 (WS): Work in pattern back to 4 (5, 6, 6, 7, 8, 8, 10, 10) sts before the end of the Left shoulder; W&T.
Short Row 3: Work in pattern to end.Short Row 4: Work in pattern to 4 (5, 6, 6, 7, 8, 8, 10, 10) sts before the wrapped st, W&T.
Next Row: Work in pattern across all sts, picking up wrapped sts and knitting them together with the sts they wrap.

Break yarn and put shoulders on st holders or scrap yarn.

Back

Place 100 (116, 130, 140, 150, 164, 176, 190, 192) Back sts back on needles, and attach yarn ready to begin a RS row. Work as for Front from ** to **. 84 (92, 104, 106, 110, 124, 130, 134, 134) sts remain.

Work 57 (56, 63, 65, 66, 70, 70, 73, 79) rows even in pattern to approximately 8.5 (8.5, 9.75, 10, 10.25, 10.75, 10.75, 11, 11.75)" above armhole bo, ending on a WS row.

On the next RS row, sts are bound off at the back neck to form the neckline.

Work in pattern across 17 (20, 23, 23, 24, 27, 29, 32, 32) sts, BO the next 50 (54, 58, 60, 62, 70, 72, 70, 70) sts, then work in pattern to the end of row.

Turn and work in pattern to 2 sts before neckline edge of left shoulder; P2tog. Attach a new ball of yarn at the right shoulder; P2tog TBL across the first 2 sts, then work in pattern to end. 15 (18, 21, 21, 22, 25, 27, 30, 30) sts remain on each shoulder.

Work short rows as for Front, working the back left shoulder as the front right and the back right as the front left, but do not break yarn.

Join Shoulders

Turn body inside out, and join the shoulders together using working yarn from the back and the 3-needle Bind-Off technique.

Finishing

Set in Sleeves

With right sides facing out, set sleeves into armhole openings, making sure that the center of each sleeve cap is placed at the shoulder seam and that the seam under the sleeve and bound off sts of the armhole are centered. Pin in place. Using yarn needle and yarn, begin at the underarm and sew sleeves into the armholes, using mattress stitch.

Collar

The collar is worked as a rolled crew neck. Use smaller needles.

With RS facing and starting at right shoulder seam, PU and K 5 sts to the bound off sts at the back neck, 52 (58, 60, 62, 64, 72, 74, 70, 70) bound off sts across the neck, 5 sts up to the left shoulder seam, and 76 (78, 82, 82, 82, 96, 96, 96, 96) sts around front neckline edge back to right shoulder. 138 (146, 152, 154, 156, 178, 180, 176, 176) sts. PM and join to work in the round.

Work in K1, P1 rib for 2". Break yarn, leaving a tail of several yards. Fold the collar towards the inside. Using the yarn tail, whipstitch the live sts to the back of the picked up row.

Weave in ends. Wash and block to measurements.

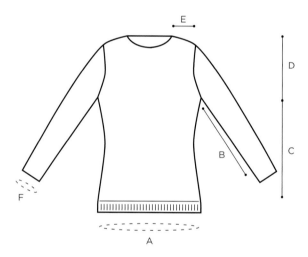

A 32 (36, 40, 44, 48, 52, 56, 60, 64)"
B 17.25 (17, 17, 18, 17.5, 17.5, 16.25, 15.25, 14)"
C 14 (14, 14.25, 14.25, 14.5, 14.5, 15, 15.5, 15.5)"
D 8.5 (9, 10, 10, 10.5, 11, 11, 11.5, 11.5)"
E 2.25 (3, 3, 3.25, 3.5, 3.75, 4, 4, 4)"
F 8.5 (8.5, 9, 10, 10.75, 11.5, 11.5, 11.5, 12.5)"

Sleeve Center

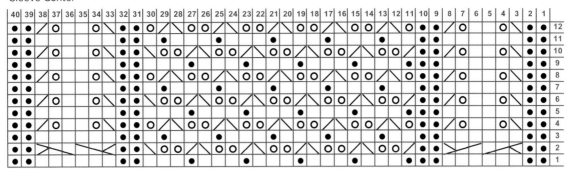

Sleeve Border Right (beginning of round)

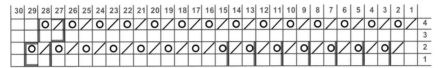

The stitch closest to the Sleeve Center (st 30 in the Right chart and st 1 in the Left chart) should always be worked in St st.

Sleeve Border Left (end of round)

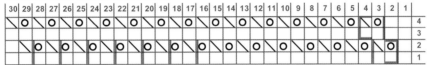

Body Pattern

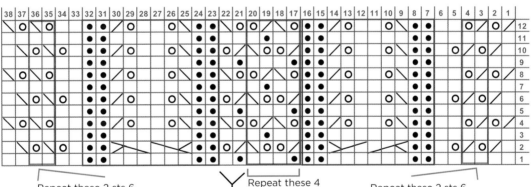

Repeat these 2 sts 6 (8, 14, 15, 18, 19, 22, 27, 30) times.

Repeat these 4 sts 14 (15, 15, 15, 16, 18, 19, 19, 19) times.

Repeat these 2 sts 6 (8, 14, 15, 18, 19, 22, 27, 30) times.

Legend

☐ **knit**
RS: knit stitch

⊡ **purl**
RS: purl stitch

◿ **k2tog**
Knit two stitches together as one stitch

⊙ **yo**
Yarn Over

◺ **ssk**
Slip one stitch as if to knit, Slip another stitch as if to knit. Insert left-hand needle into front of these 2 stitches and knit them together

c3 over 3 right
sl3 to CN, hold in back. k3, then k3 from CN

c3 over 3 left
sl3 to CN, hold in front. k3, k3 from CN

CONTOUR TUNIC

by Kerin Dimeler-Laurence

FINISHED MEASUREMENTS

32 (36, 40, 44, 48, 52, 56, 60, 64)"
finished chest measurement. Garment is
meant to be worn with 1-2" of positive
ease.

YARN

Knit Picks *Wool of the Andes Tweed* (80%
Peruvian Highland Wool, 20% Donegal
Tweed; 110 yards/50g): Reindeer Heather
25962, 16 (17, 19, 21, 23, 27, 28, 30, 31)
balls.

NEEDLES

US 8 (5mm) DPNs and 24-48" circular
needles, or long circulars for Magic Loop,
or size to obtain gauge

US 7 (4.5mm) DPNs and 24-48" circular
needles, or long circulars for Magic Loop,
one size smaller than those used to
obtain gauge

NOTIONS

Tapestry Needle
Stitch markers
Scrap yarn or stitch holders
Cable Needle

GAUGE

24 sts and 28 rounds = 4" over cable
pattern, blocked.

Contour Tunic

Notes:

All references to *Right* and *Left* are as worn, unless otherwise noted.

Seed Stitch (worked in the round)

Rnd 1: *K1, P1, rep from *, ending with K1 if working over an odd number of sts.

Rnd 2: *P1, K1, rep from *, ending with P1 if working over an odd number of sts.

Rep Rnds 1-2 for pattern

DIRECTIONS

This tunic is worked from the bottom up in the round. Shaping is worked around the center cable panel, giving it a slimming silhouette. Sleeves are worked from the bottom-up and joined to the body at the yoke. Raglan shoulders lead into a deep collar.

Sleeves (Make two)

The sleeves begin in the round at the wrist and are increased to the underarm. They are then joined to the Body at the Yoke. Make two identical sleeves.

With smaller needles, CO 48 (48, 52, 56, 60, 64, 68, 68, 72) sts. PM and join to work in the round, being careful not to twist sts. Work in K2, P2 rib for 2". Switch to larger needles.

Begin Sleeve pattern and increases on next round.

Sleeve Pattern

On the next round, begin working from round 1 of the Sleeve chart, beginning and ending at the marks for your size. Continue working repeats of these 16 rounds throughout the length of the sleeve.

Sleeve Increases

The sleeves are increased to the underarms in the seed stitch sections. Work all new sts in Seed st as established.

Increase Round: KFB, work in pattern to last st, KFB. 2 sts increased.

Sizes 48", 56" and 64" only: Work an Increase Round on the next round.

All Sizes: Work an Increase Round every 6th (6th, 6th, 6th, 6th, 4th, 5th, 4th, [5th and 9th]) round 19 (19, 18, 20, 19, 25, 22, 24, 11) times. Work 8 (8, 12, 0, 3, 10, 0, 14, 6) rounds in pattern.

86 (86, 88, 96, 100, 114, 114, 116, 118) sts on the needles. Place sleeve on scrap yarn or stitch holder, and work second sleeve to this point.

Body

The body begins with the same ribbing as the sleeves and is shaped over the waist.

With smaller needles, CO 220 (248, 268, 300, 320, 348, 360, 396, 424) sts. PM and join to work in the round, being careful not to twist sts. Work in K2, P2 rib for 4"; place a marker after 110 (124, 134, 150, 160, 174, 180, 198, 212) sts to mark right underarm. Switch to larger needles.

On the next round, set up body patterning:

Setup Rnd: *Work 5 (7, 5, 7, 9, 11, 13, 15, 17) sts in Seed St, PM, work from Left Braid over the next 21 sts, PM, work from Pine Bark Body Setup chart over the next 58 (68, 82, 94, 100, 110, 112, 126, 136) sts, following repeat instructions in the chart, PM, work from Right Braid over the next 21 sts, PM, work 5 (7, 5, 7, 9, 11, 13, 15, 17) sts in Seed St, rep from * once more.

Work in pattern as established for 2 (1, 2, 7, 12, 20, 22, 22, 22) rounds.

Waist Shaping

Begin working from Pine Bark Decrease chart, following directions for your size, and maintaining the seed st and Braid panels, over the next 67 (67, 73, 73, 73, 73, 73, 73, 73) rounds. 164 (188, 208, 240, 260, 288, 300, 336, 364) sts on the needles. After completing the Pine Bark Decrease chart, move on to the Pine Bark Increase chart, and follow directions for your size. 192 (216, 240, 264, 288, 312, 336, 360, 384) sts on the needles.

Yoke

On the next round, the sleeves are joined to the body and the yoke is knit in the round to the neckline.

Next Rnd: Work across the front of the body to 4 (4, 5, 5, 6, 6, 6, 7, 7) sts before right underarm marker. K1, PM. Slide the next 6 (6, 8, 8, 10, 10, 10, 12, 12) body sts onto scrap yarn or a stitch holder.

Place one sleeve back onto spare needles, leaving the first and last 3 (3, 4, 4, 5, 5, 5, 6, 6) sts of the round on the scrap yarn or stitch holder. Work directly from the body around the sleeve, working the first and last sts as K sts. PM, and knit the first live st of the back of the body; this joins the sleeve.

Work across the back of the body in pattern to 4 (4, 5, 5, 6, 6, 6, 7, 7) sts before the end of round (left underarm). K1, PM. Slide the last 3 (3, 4, 4, 5, 5, 5, 6, 6) sts of this round and the first 3 (3, 4, 4, 5, 5, 5, 6, 6) sts of the next onto scrap yarn or a stitch holder. Place the second sleeve on spare needles, leaving 6 (6, 8, 8, 10, 10, 10, 12, 12) sts on the holder as done for the first sleeve. K1 and work around sleeve in pattern to last st, K1; PM. This marks the new beginning of round. Knit directly into first live st of body; this joins the sleeve and begins the next round. 340 (364, 384, 424, 444, 500, 524, 544, 272) sts on the needles.

Work around all sts, knitting the sts next to each marker and working between them in pattern as established, for 3 rounds, placing marker after the first 45 (51, 56, 62, 67, 79, 84, 90) sts to mark center front. This marker is not noted in Raglan Shaping, but will be used to shape the neckline.

Raglan Shaping

The yoke of the sweater is shaped to the neckline with raglan decreases. Neckline and decreases are worked at the same time – read both sections before proceeding. A table is included to keep track of all shaping that occurs on each round.

Raglan Decrease Round: *SSK, work in pattern to 2 sts before raglan marker, K2tog, SM; repeat from * around body; 8 sts decreased.

Sleeve Decrease Round: *Work in pattern to raglan marker, SM, SSK, work in pattern to 2 sts before raglan marker, K2tog, SM; repeat from * around body; 4 sts decreased.

Body Decrease Round: *SSK, work in pattern to 2 sts before underarm marker, K2tog, SM, work in pattern to next underarm marker, SM; repeat from * around body; 4 sts decreased.

Each Round listed in this chart is a round of the yoke. Read from the bottom up, working decreases on the rounds noted and working plain where there is no decrease noted.

Maintain the sts on either side of each marker as knit sts throughout yoke. As you decrease sts in the cabled sections of the patterns, only work cables that have enough sts to be completed; work those with too few sts as St st.

Neckline

The beginning of the neckline is marked by a pink box on the Raglan Shaping table. On this row (or, if this is not a cabled row, the next row), sts are bound off at the front neck to form the neckline.

Work in pattern to 4 (4, 4, 4, 4, 5, 5, 5, 5) sts before the center front marker. BO the next 10 (10, 10, 10, 10, 12, 12, 12, 12) sts, removing marker; work in pattern to the end of the round, then work to 3 sts before the first bound off st of the neckline, K3tog. You are now working flat, with the row beginning and ending at the neckline edge. Follow neckline decrease directions together with Raglan shaping, as indicated in the table.

Neckline Double Decrease Row:

RS: Work in pattern to last 3 sts of left neck edge, SSSK. K3tog, work in pattern across right shoulder.
WS: Work in pattern to last 3 sts of right neck edge, P3tog. P3tog TBL, work in pattern across left shoulder.

Neckline Single Decrease Row:

RS: Work in pattern to last 2 sts of left neck edge, SSK. K2tog, work in pattern across right shoulder.
WS: Work in pattern to last 2 sts of right neck edge, P2tog. P2tog TBL, work in pattern across left shoulder.

Shape Neckline:

Work a Neckline Double Decrease Row every row 2 (2, 2, 1, 1, 3, 3, 3, 3) times; work a Neckline Decrease Row every row 4 (4, 4, 7, 7, 6, 6, 6, 6) times, then every other row 1 (2, 2, 2, 2, 2, 2, 2, 2) times, work 3 rows in pattern, work a Neckline Decrease Row.

Follow Raglan shaping to end. 1 st should remain on either side of the front, 10 (10, 12, 12, 12, 14, 14, 14, 14) sts on each shoulder, and 34 (36, 36, 38, 38, 46, 46, 46, 46) sts across the back neck; 56 (58, 62, 64, 64, 76, 76, 76, 76) sts overall.

Collar

The collar is worked flat and opens along the raglan edge for an asymmetric finish.

With smaller needles, CO 6 sts. Immediately after the CO sts, with RS facing and starting at the raglan seam at the left side of the neckline, PU and K 42 (46, 46, 50, 50, 58, 58, 58, 58) sts across the front neck to the first live st on the right shoulder; knit across

live sts on the shoulders and back. 104 (110, 114, 120, 120, 140, 140, 140, 140) sts.

Work in K2, P2 rib for 10". BO all sts loosely in rib. With the cast on tail from the collar, whipstitch the six cast on stitches behind the first six collar stitches across the split.

Finishing

Graft the live sts at the underarms. Weave in ends. Wash and block to measurements.

	32	36	40	44	48	52	56	60	64
85									R
84								R	R
83								R	R
82								R	B
81						R	R	R	R
80						R	R	B	B
79						R	R	R	R
78						B	B	B	B
77						R	R	R	R
76						R	R	B	B
75						R	R	R	R
74							B	B	B
73						R	R	R	R
72						B	B	B	B
71						R	R	R	R
70								B	
69						R	R	R	R
68					R		B		B
67					R	R	R	R	R
66					B			B	
65				R	R	R	R	R	R
64				R	R		B		B
63				R	R	R	R	R	R
62				B	B			B	
61				R	R	R	R	R	R
60			R	R	B			R	B
59			R	R	R	R	R	R	R
58			B					B	
57			R	R	R	R	R	R	R
56			R	B	B				B
55			R	R	R	R	R	R	R
54	S	R	B	B					
53	R	R	R	R	R	R	R	R	R
52	S	R			B				B
51	R	R	R	R	R	R	R	R	R
50		S							
49	R	R	R	R	R	R	R	R	R
48	S								
47	R	R	R	R	R	R	R	R	R
46		R							
45	R	R	R	R	R	R	R	R	R
44									
43	R	R	R	R	R	R	R	R	R
42									
41	R	R	R	R	R	R	R	R	R
40									

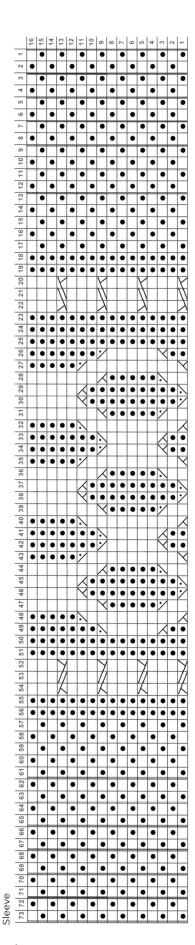

Sleeve

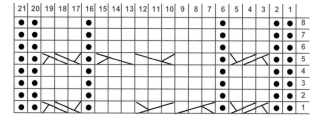

Right Braid

Left Braid

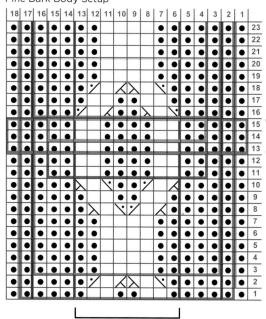

Pine Bark Body Setup

Repeat these 8 sts a total of 6 (8, 9, 11, 12, 13, 13, 15, 16) times.

Sizes 32 and 36: Move on to round 9 of the Pine Bark Decrease chart.

Pine Bark Decrease

Repeat these 8 sts a total of 2 (4, 5, 7, 8, 9, 9, 11, 12) times.

Pine Bark Increase

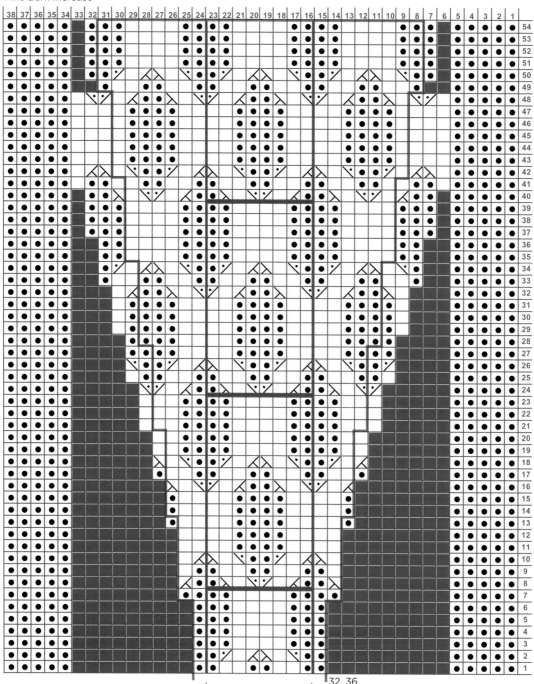

Repeat these 8 sts a total of 2 (4, 5, 7, 8, 9, 9, 11, 12) times.

Pine Bark Yoke

Chart columns (top): 38 37 36 35 34 33 32 31 30 29 28 27 26 25 24 23 22 21 20 19 18 17 16 15 14 13 12 11 10 9 8 7 6 5 4 3 2 1

Chart rows (right side): 28 27 26 25 24 23 22 21 20 19 18 17 16 15 14 13 12 11 10 9 8 7 6 5 4 3 2 1

Legend

Symbol	Name	Instruction
●	purl	purl stitch
c1 over 2 right		sl2 to CN, hold in back. k1, k2 from CN
c3 over 3 right		sl3 to CN, hold in back. k3, then k3 from CN
☐	knit	knit stitch
c1 over 2 left		sl 1 to CN, hold in front. k2, k1 from CN
c3 over 3 left		sl3 to CN, hold in front. k3, k3 from CN
⊡	p2tog tbl	Purl two stitches together in back loops, inserting needle from the left, behind and into the backs of the 2nd & 1st stitches in that order
■	No Stitch	Placeholder - No stitch made.
c2 over 1 right P		sl1 to CN, hold in back. k2, p1 from CN
c2 over 1 left P		sl2 to CN, hold in front. p1, k2 from CN
⊿	p2tog	Purl 2 stitches together

Line legend:
- 32"
- 36"
- 40"
- 44"
- 48"
- 52"
- 56"
- 60"
- 64"

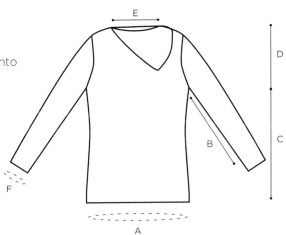

A 32 (36, 40, 44, 48, 52, 56, 60, 64)"
B 19.5 (19.5, 19, 19.25, 19, 17.75, 17.25, 17.75, 17.25)"
C 21.25 (21.5, 22.5, 22.75, 23.75, 24, 24.25, 24, 23.5)"
D 7 (7, 7.75, 8.5, 9, 10.5, 10.5, 11, 11.25)"
E 5.75 (6, 6.25, 6.25, 6.5, 7.75, 7.75, 7.25, 7.25)"
F 7.75 (8, 8.75, 9.5, 9.75, 11, 11.25, 11.5, 12)"

CUMBRIA SWEATER

by Kerin Dimeler-Laurence

FINISHED MEASUREMENTS

32 (36, 40, 44, 48, 52, 56, 60, 64)"
finished chest measurement

YARN

Knit Picks Wool of the Andes Superwash
(100% Superwash Peruvian Highland
Wool; 110 yards/50g): Dove Heather
26302, 10 (11, 12, 13, 14, 15, 16, 17, 18) balls.

NEEDLES

US 8 (5 mm) DPNs and 24-48" circular
needles, or long circulars for Magic Loop,
or size to obtain gauge

US 7 (4.5 mm) DPNs and 24-48" circular
needles, or long circular needles for
Magic Loop one size smaller than those
used to obtain gauge

NOTIONS

Tapestry Needle
Stitch markers
Scrap yarn or stitch holders

GAUGE

19 sts and 25 rows = 4" in St st in the
round, blocked.

Cumbria Sweater

Notes:

Inspired by traditional fishermen's ganseys, this pullover features a textured pattern on the yoke and sleeves. The sleeves are knit in the round from the cuff up to the sleeve cap where it is knit flat. The pullover body is knit from the hem up in the round to the armholes. All references to *Right* and *Left* are as worn, unless otherwise noted.

Twisted Rib (worked in the round, over an even number of sts)
All Rnds: (K1 TBL, P1) around.

Moss Stitch (worked in the round, over an even number of sts)
Rows 1 and 2: (K1, P1) across.
Rows 3 and 4: (P1, K1) across.

Three-needle Bind Off
Hold the two pieces of knitting together with the points of the needles facing to the right. Insert a third needle into the first stitch on each of the needles knitwise, starting with the front needle. Work a knit stitch, pulling the loop through both of the stitches you've inserted the third needle through. After you've pulled the loop through, slip the first stitch off of each of the needles. This takes two stitches (one from the front needle and one from the back) and joins them to make one finished stitch on the third needle (held in your right hand). Repeat this motion, inserting your needle into one stitch on the front and back needles, knitting them together and slipping them off of the needles. Each time you complete a second stitch, pass the first finished stitch over the second and off of the needle (as you would in a traditional bind-off).

DIRECTIONS
Sleeves (Make 2)
The sleeves are worked in the round from the wrist to the underarm. They are then worked flat.

With smaller needles, CO 46 (46, 48, 52, 56, 60, 60, 60, 64) sts. Join to work in the round, being careful not to twist sts. PM to indicate beginning of round.

Work in Twisted rib for 2".

Start sleeve pattern
Set-up Rnd: K10 (10, 11, 13, 15, 17, 17, 17, 19), PM, work row 1 of Sleeve Chart over next 27 sts, PM, K to 1 st before end, M1R, K1. 47 (47, 49, 53, 57, 61, 61, 61, 65) sts

Continuing in pattern as established, work Sleeve Chart in between markers and St st on either side of the markers, for 3 rounds.

Work Inc Rnd: K1, M1L, work in pattern to last st, M1R, K1. 49 (49, 51, 55, 59, 63, 63, 63, 67) sts

Continuing in pattern, work Inc Rnd every 9th (8th, 6th, 7th, 7th, 6th, 5th, 5th, 5th) round 10 (11, 15, 13, 14, 16, 16, 17, 15) more times. 69 (71, 81, 81, 87, 95, 95, 97, 97) sts

Work 5 (6, 6, 10, 1, 4, 12, 2, 4) rounds in pattern.

Sleeve Cap
Continuing in Sleeve Chart pattern between markers, shape sleeve cap: Stitches are bound off at the base of the sleeve cap. The cap is then worked flat to the end.

Work to 3 (3, 3, 3, 3, 4, 4, 5, 4) sts before the end of the round. BO the last 3 (3, 3, 3, 3, 4, 4, 5, 4) sts of the round, then the first 5 (5, 5, 5, 5, 6, 6, 7, 6) sts of the next round.
Knit to the last 3 sts of the round, SSSK. You are now working flat over 59 (61, 71, 71, 77, 83, 83, 83, 85) sts.

Double Decrease Row:
RS: K3tog, work in pattern to last 3 sts, SSSK
WS: P3tog, work in pattern to last 3 sts, P3tog TBL

Single Decrease Row:
RS: K2tog, work in pattern to last 2 sts, SSK.
WS: P2tog, work in pattern to last 2 sts, P2tog TBL

Work a Double Decrease Row every row 1 (1, 1, 1, 1, 1, 1, 2, 2) times.
Work a Single Decrease Row every row 5 (4, 4, 5, 6, 6, 6, 3, 2) times,
then every other row 5 (6, 5, 5, 5, 6, 5, 4, 4) times,
then every third row 3 (3, 3, 7, 7, 6, 10, 14, 16) times,
then every other row 2 (2, 6, 3, 2, 3, 3, 3, 3) times,
then every row 3 (3, 4, 1, 4, 5, 2, 2, 2) times.
Work a Double Decrease Row every row 2 (1, 1, 2, 2, 2, 2, 1, 1) times. 15 (17, 19, 17, 17, 19, 19, 19, 19) sts
BO all remaining sts.

Body
The body begins with the same ribbing as the sleeves.

With smaller needles, CO 150 (170, 190, 210, 230, 246, 266, 286, 302) sts. PM and join to work in the round, being careful not to twist sts.

Work in Twisted rib for 2" or desired length; place a marker after 75 (85, 95, 105, 115, 123, 133, 143, 151) sts to mark right underarm.

Switch to larger needles. You may now choose to work the body with Straight Sides (no shaping), or with Waist Shaping.

Straight Sides
Work evenly in St st in the round until body measures 14 (14, 14.25, 14.25, 14.5, 14.5, 15, 15.5, 15.5)" from Twisted Rib, or desired length.

Proceed to Seed Stitch Band section.

Shaped Sides
If you want to add basic waist shaping, these directions will give a subtle, relaxed fit.

Work 5 (5, 6, 6, 8, 8, 11, 14, 14) rounds in St st.

Work Dec Rnd: *K2, SSK, K to 4 sts before marker, K2tog, K2*, SM; repeat between *s around. 4 sts decreased.

Then work Dec Rnd every 10th round 4 times. 130 (150, 170, 190, 210, 226, 246, 266, 282) sts

Work 5 rounds even in St st (for waist).

Work Inc Rnd: *K2, M1L, K to 2 sts before marker, M1R, K2*, SM;

repeat between *s around. 4 sts increased.

Then work Inc Rnd every 9th round 2 times. 150 (170, 190, 210, 230, 246, 266, 286, 302) sts

Work 2 rounds in St st or until body measures 14 (14, 14.25, 14.25, 14. 5, 14. 5, 15, 15.5, 15.5)" from Twisted Rib, or desired length.

Seed Stitch Band:
Rnd 1: *P 11 (16, 21, 26, 31, 35, 40, 45, 49), PM to mark yoke patterning, P53, PM to mark yoke patterning, P to underarm marker, rep from * once more to beginning of round marker.
Rnds 2 and 3: (K1, P1) around.
Rnds 4 and 5: (P1, K1) around.
Rnd 6: Purl to 2 (3, 4, 4, 5, 6, 9, 12, 13) sts before end of rnd.

Divide for Front and Back
On the next round, stitches are bound off at each armhole and Yoke patterning is begun. After this, the Front and Back are worked flat separately to the shoulders. All armhole decreases take place over the Moss stitch sections.

Set-up Rnd: * BO the next 4 (6, 8, 8, 10, 12, 18, 24, 26) sts, removing marker. .Work in Moss st to marker, SM, work Row 1 of Yoke chart, SM. * work in Moss st to 2 (3, 4, 4, 5, 6, 9, 12, 13) sts before the underarm marker. Rep from * to *. Do not break yarn. 71 (79, 87, 97, 105, 111, 115, 119, 125) sts remain across both Front and Back.

Front
Place Back sts on scrap yarn or a stitch holder, and work flat across Front sts only.

Armhole Shaping:
Armhole Double Decrease Row:
RS: K3tog, work in pattern to last 3 sts, SSSK.
WS: P3tog TBL, work in pattern to last 3 sts, P3tog.

Armhole Single Decrease Row:
RS: K2tog, K to last 2 sts, SSK.
WS: P2tog TBL, P to last 2 sts, P2tog.

** Work Armhole Double Decrease Row 0 (0, 0, 1, 1, 2, 2, 3, 4) times.
Work Armhole Single Decrease Row 1 (1, 3, 2, 3, 3, 5, 3, 5) times.
[Work 1 (2, 1, 1, 1, 1, 1, 1, 1) rows even and then Single Decrease Row once] - 1 (1, 2, 2, 3, 3, 4, 6, 4) times.
[Work 2 rows even and then Single Decrease Row once] – 1 (1, 1, 2, 2, 4, 1, 1, 2) times.
[Work 4 (4, 5, 3, 3, 5, 3, 4, 4) rows even and then Single Decrease Row once] – once.
[Work 6 (12, 6, 6, 4, -, 4, -, -) rows even and then Single Decrease Row once] – 1 (1, 1, 1, 2, 0, 1, 0, 0) times. 61 (69, 71, 77, 79, 81, 83, 85, 85) sts **

Work 14 (11, 21, 20, 18, 21, 27, 29, 32) rows in pattern.

Neckline
On the next RS row, sts are bound off at the front neck to form the neckline.

Work in pattern across the first 27 (31, 31, 34, 35, 36, 37, 38, 38) sts, BO the next 7 (7, 9, 9, 9, 9, 9, 9, 9) sts; work in pattern to end.

Attach a second ball of yarn at the left neckline edge and work both sides of the neckline together, following Shape Neckline directions below.

Neckline Double Decrease Row:
RS: Work in pattern to last 3 sts of left neck edge, SSSK. K3tog across first 3 sts of right neck edge, work in pattern across right shoulder.
WS: Work in pattern to last 3 sts of right neck edge, P3tog. P3tog TBL across first 3 sts of left neck edge, work in pattern across left shoulder.

Neckline Single Decrease Row:
RS: Work in pattern to last 2 sts of left neck edge, SSK. K2tog across first 2 sts of right neck edge, work in pattern across right shoulder.
WS: Work in pattern to last 2 sts of right neck edge, P2tog. P2tog TBL across first 2 sts of left neck edge, work in pattern across left shoulder

Shape Neckline:
Continuing in established pattern, work Neckline Double Decrease Row every row 3 (3, 3, 4, 4, 4, 4, 4) times, then work Neckline Single Decrease Row every row 7 (7, 7, 6, 6, 6, 6, 8, 8) times, then every other row 4 (4, 4, 4, 4, 4, 3, 3) times. 17 (17, 17, 18, 18, 18, 18, 19, 19) sts have been removed from each front; 10 (14, 14, 16, 17, 18, 19, 19, 19) sts remain on each shoulder.

Work 2 rows in pattern.

Short rows
A set of short rows finishes off the shoulders. Work each shoulder separately.

Right Shoulder
Short Row 1 (RS): Work to 4 (5, 5, 5, 7, 7, 7, 6) sts before the end, W&T.
Short Row 2 (WS): Work in pattern to end of row.
Short Row 3: Work to 4 (5, 5, 5, 7, 7, 7, 6) sts before the last wrapped st, W&T.
Short Row 4: Work in pattern to end of row.
Final Row: Turn and work across all sts, picking up wrapped sts and knitting them together with the sts they wrap.

Break yarn and put shoulders on st holders or scrap yarn.

Left Shoulder
Short Row 1 (RS): Work in pattern to end of row.
Short Row 2 (WS): Work to 4 (5, 5, 5, 7, 7, 7, 6) sts before the end, W&T.
Short Row 3: Work in pattern to end of row.
Short Row 4: Work to 4 (5, 5, 5, 7, 7, 7, 6) sts before the last wrapped st, W&T.
Final Row: Turn and work across all sts, picking up wrapped sts and knitting them together with the sts they wrap.

Break yarn and put shoulders on st holders or scrap yarn.

Back
Place 71 (79, 87, 97, 105, 111, 115, 119, 125) held Back sts on needles, and attach yarn ready to begin a WS row.

Work through Armhole shaping directions from ** to ** as for Front. 61 (69, 71, 79, 81, 81, 83, 85, 85) sts.

Work 32 (29, 39, 38, 36, 39, 45, 47, 50) rows in pattern.

On the next RS row, sts are bound off at the back neck to form the neckline.

Work in pattern across 11 (15, 15, 17, 18, 19, 20, 20, 20) sts, BO the next 41 (41, 43, 43, 45, 45, 45, 47, 47) sts, then work in pattern to the end of row. A set of short rows finishes off the shoulders. Work each shoulder separately.

Short Rows
Left Shoulder
First Row (WS): Turn and work in pattern to 2 sts before neckline edge of left shoulder; P2tog.
Short Row 1 (RS): Work to 4 (5, 5, 5, 7, 7, 7, 7, 6) sts before the end, W&T.
Short Row 2 (WS): Work in pattern to end of row.
Short Row 3: Work to 4 (5, 5, 5, 7, 7, 7, 7, 6) sts before the last wrapped st, W&T.
Short Row 4: Work in pattern to end of row.
Final Row: Turn and work across all sts, picking up wrapped sts and knitting them together with the sts they wrap. Do not break yarn,

Right Shoulder
Attach a new ball of yarn at the right shoulder neckline;
First Row (WS): P2tog TBL across the first 2 sts, then work in pattern to end.
Short Row 1 (RS): Work in pattern to end of row.
Short Row 2 (WS): Work to 4 (5, 5, 5, 7, 7, 7, 7, 6) sts before the end, W&T.
Short Row 3: Work in pattern to end of row.
Short Row 4: Work to 4 (5, 5, 5, 7, 7, 7, 7, 6) sts before the last wrapped st, W&T.
Final Row: Turn and work across all sts, picking up wrapped sts and knitting them together with the sts they wrap. Do not break yarn.

Join Shoulders
Turn body inside out, and join the shoulders together using working yarn from the back and the 3-needle Bind-Off technique.

Finishing
Set in Sleeves
With right sides facing out, set sleeves into armhole openings, making sure that the center of each sleeve cap is placed at the shoulder seam and that the seam under the sleeve and bound off sts of the armhole are centered. Pin in place. Using yarn needle and yarn, begin at the underarm and sew sleeves into the armholes, using mattress stitch.

Collar
The collar is worked as a rolled crew neck.

Using smaller needles, with RS facing and starting at right shoulder seam, PU and K 3 sts to the bound off sts at the back neck, 41 (41, 43, 43, 45, 45, 45, 47, 47) bound off sts across the neck, 3 sts up to the left shoulder seam, and 43 (43, 45, 45, 47, 47,

49, 49, 49) sts around front neckline edge back to right shoulder. 90 (90, 94, 94, 98, 98, 100, 102, 102) sts. PM and join to work in the round.

Work in Twisted rib for 2". Break yarn, leaving a tail of several yards. Fold the collar towards the inside. Using the yarn tail, whipstitch the live sts to the back of the picked up row.

Weave in ends. Wash and block to measurements.

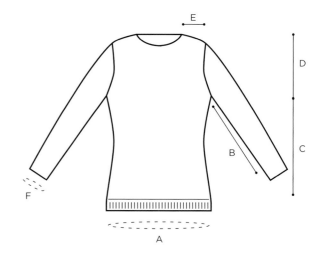

A 32 (36, 40, 44, 48, 52, 56, 60, 64)"
B 17.25 (17, 17, 18, 17.5, 17.5, 16.25, 15.25, 14)"
C 14 (14, 14.25, 14.25, 14.5, 14.5, 15, 15.5, 15.5)"
D 8.5 (9, 10, 10, 10.5, 11, 11, 11.5, 11.5)"
E 2.25 (3, 3, 3.25, 3.5, 3.75, 4, 4, 4)"
F 8.5 (8.5, 9, 10, 10.75, 11.5, 11.5, 11.5, 12.5)"

Yoke

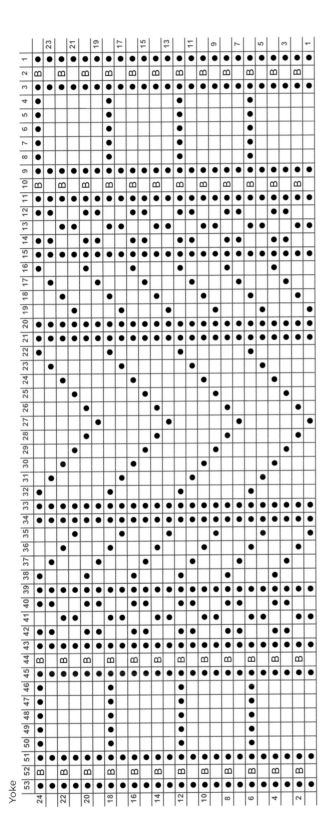

Sleeve

Legend

	purl
⊙	RS: purl stitch WS: knit stitch
☐	knit RS: knit stitch WS: purl stitch
B	knit tbl RS: Knit stitch through back loop WS: Purl stitch through back loop

KEIGHLEY HAT AND SCARF

by Kerin Dimeler-Laurence

FINISHED MEASUREMENTS

Scarf: 8x70"
Hat Circumference: 19"

YARN

Knit Picks Wool of the Andes (100% Peruvian Highland Wool; 110 yards/50g): MC Mink Heather 24279, 9 balls, CC Red 23764, 1 ball.

NEEDLES

US 8 (5mm) straight or circular needles, or size to obtain gauge
US 7 (4.5mm) DPNs or long circular needles for Magic Loop , or size to obtain gauge

NOTIONS

Tapestry Needle
Stitch markers
Cable needle

GAUGE

24 sts and 26 rows = 4" over pattern worked flat on larger needles, blocked.
26 sts and 29 rows = 4" over pattern worked in the round on smaller needles, blocked.

Keighley Hat and Scarf

Covered in traveling cables and full of rich texture, this warm set is named after a small town in Yorkshire, England. The hat features a red pom-pom that finishes the crown. Make it bigger or smaller as your heart desires.

DIRECTIONS

Scarf

With MC and using larger needles, CO 50 sts.
Begin working from Row 1 of the Scarf Chart.
Work 11 repeats of these 40 rows.
BO all sts.
Wash and block.

Hat

With MC and smaller needles, CO 120 sts. PM and join to work in the rnd, being careful not to twist sts.
Begin working from Rnd 1 of the Hat Chart.
Work through to the end of the chart.

After finishing the last round, break yarn leaving 12" tail. Using a yarn needle, pass the yarn tail through the remaining live sts and pull tight to BO. Do not trim this tail yet; it will be used to attach the pom-pom.

Finishing

With CC, make a pompom with a diameter of about 2.5".
Using the yarn tail on the crown of the hat, sew the pompom to the hat, making several passes over the binding yarn of the pompom.
Weave in ends.
Wash and block to measurements.

Scarf Chart

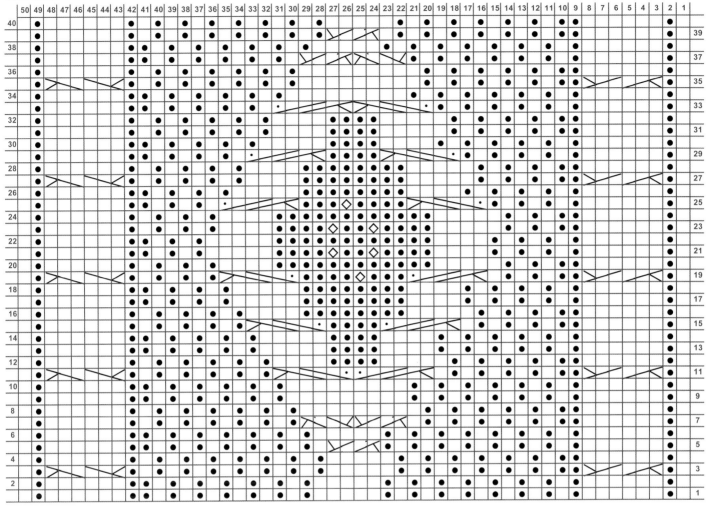

Legend

purl
RS: purl stitch
WS: knit stitch

knit
RS: knit stitch
WS: purl stitch

c2 over 4 right P
sl4 to CN, hold in back. k2 then p4 from CN

bobble
To make bobble: (k1 p1 k1 p1 k1) in one stitch, turn and p5. Turn and sl3-k2tog-psso, completing bobble

c2 over 4 left P
sl2 to CN, hold in front. p4, k2 from CN

c2 over 2 left
sl 2 to CN, hold in front. k2, k2 from CN

c2 over 2 right
sl2 to CN, hold in back. k2, k2 from CN

c3 over 3 right
sl3 to CN, hold in back. k3, then k3 from CN

c3 over 3 left
sl3 to CN, hold in front. k3, k3 from CN

No Stitch
Placeholder - No stitch made.

p2tog
RS: Purl 2 stitches together
WS: Knit 2 stitches together

k2tog
RS: Knit two stitches together as one stitch
WS: Purl 2 stitches together

Central Double Dec
Slip first and second stitches together as if to k2tog. Knit 1 stitch. Pass two slipped stitches over the knit stitch.

Hat Chart

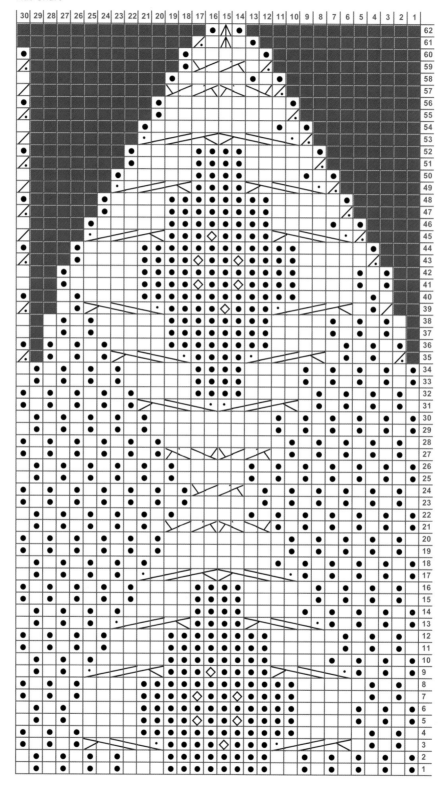

FIDDLEHEAD CARDIGAN

by Kerin Dimeler-Laurence

FINISHED MEASUREMENTS

32 (36, 40, 44, 48, 52, 56, 60, 64)"
finished bust measurement

YARN

Knit Picks Wool of the Andes Tweed (80%
Peruvian Highland Wool, 20% Donegal
Tweed; 110 yards/50g): Dill Heather
25456, 9 (10, 11, 12, 13, 14, 15, 16, 17) balls.

NEEDLES

US 7 (4.5mm) DPNs and 24-48" circular
needles, or long circulars for Magic Loop,
or size to obtain gauge

NOTIONS

Tapestry Needle
Stitch markers
Scrap yarn or stitch holders
7 0.75" buttons

GAUGE

25 sts and 27 rows = 4" in Fiddlehead
Cable pattern, blocked.
19 sts and 27 rows = 4" in Diamond
Brocade pattern, blocked.

Fiddlehead Cardigan

Notes:

Named after a fern that uncurls slowly as it grows, this cardigan features beautiful, bold cables for textural appeal and pockets to hold all of your woodland treasures. The garment body is knit from the hem up and the sleeves from the cuff up. All references to *Right* and *Left* are as worn, unless otherwise noted.

Three-needle Bind Off

Hold the two pieces of knitting together with the points of the needles facing to the right. Insert a third needle into the first stitch on each of the needles knitwise, starting with the front needle. Work a knit stitch, pulling the loop through both of the stitches you've inserted the third needle through. After you've pulled the loop through, slip the first stitch off of each of the needles. This takes two stitches (one from the front needle and one from the back) and joins them to make one finished stitch on the third needle (held in your right hand). Repeat this motion, inserting your needle into one stitch on the front and back needles, knitting them together and slipping them off of the needles. Each time you complete a second stitch, pass the first finished stitch over the second and off of the needle (as you would in a traditional bind-off).

Buttonhole (worked over 11 buttonhole band sts)

This garment has unisex shaping, and so buttonholes can be worked on either side.

Buttonhole Row (WS): (P1, K1) twice, P2tog, YO twice, K2tog, P1, K1, P1.

Next Row (RS): (K1, P1) twice, (K1, P1) into the double YO, (K1, P1) twice, K1.

DIRECTIONS
Sleeves (Make two)

The sleeves begin at the wrist with a ribbed cuff.

CO 52 (52, 54, 58, 60, 64, 66, 66, 66) sts. Join to work in the round, being careful not to twist sts.

Work in K1, P1 rib for 2".

Begin working from Sleeve chart, beginning and ending the first round at the marks noted for your size. The 6-round repeats of the Diamond Brocade and 20-round repeats of the Fiddlehead motif are worked for the remainder of the sleeve.

Work without increasing until sleeve measures 6.75 (6.25, 6.25, 6.75, 8, 7, 6.25, 4.5, 3.5)" from cast on edge.
From here, the sleeves are lightly increased to the underarm. As you increase, work the new stitches in the Diamond Brocade pattern.

For each increase round, make one increase just after the first st and the other just before the last st of the rnd.

Increase every 4 (4, 4, 4, 3, 3, 3, 3, 3) rnds 16 (17, 18, 19, 22, 24, 24, 24, 24) times. 84 (86, 90, 96, 104, 112, 114, 114, 114) sts.

Work 3 rounds in pattern.

Sleeve Cap Shaping

The sleeve cap should begin on what will be a WS (odd-numbered on the chart) row; work an extra round if needed to be ready to work a WS row. On the next round, stitches are bound off at the base of the sleeve cap. The cap is then worked flat (back and forth) to the end.

Work to 4 (3, 5, 4, 4, 5, 5, 5, 5) sts before the end of the round. BO the last 4 (3, 5, 4, 4, 5, 5, 5, 5) sts of the round, then the first 6 (5, 7, 6, 6, 7, 7, 7, 7) sts of the next round. Work in pattern (an even-numbered pattern row) to the last 3 sts of the row, SSSK. You are now working flat over 70 (74, 82, 86, 90, 94, 96, 98, 98) sts.

Double Decrease Row (2 sts decreased at each edge)
RS: K3tog, work in pattern to last 3 sts, SSSK.
WS: P3tog TBL, work in pattern to last 3 sts, P3tog.

Single Decrease Row (1 st decreased at each edge)
RS: K2tog , work in pattern to last 2 sts, SSK.
WS: P2tog TBL, work in pattern to last 2 sts, P3tog.

Work a Double Decrease Row every row 1 (2, 0, 1, 2, 2, 2, 2, 2) times;
work a Single Decrease Row every row 8 (4, 6, 7, 7, 8, 7, 6, 3) times,
then every other row 8 (3, 7, 3, 6, 4, 7, 6, 5) times,
then every third row 0 (3, 2, 3, 2, 2, 3, 9, 12) times,
then every other row 0 (3, 2, 3, 2, 5, 4, 3, 5) times,
then every row 2 (3, 3, 6, 7, 8, 7, 4, 3) times;
work a Double Decrease Row every row 2 (3, 3, 3, 3, 3, 3, 3, 3) times.

After the last row of the Sleeve Cap, BO the 24 remaining sts.

Pockets (Make 2)

Two pocket flaps are knitted, set aside, and then worked into the body. CO 22 (22, 25, 25, 27, 27, 29, 32, 32) sts. Work in St st until piece measures 4.5 (4.5, 5, 5, 5.5, 5.5, 6, 6.5, 6.5)". Break yarn, leaving a 36" tail for sewing the pocket in place. Place all sts on scrap yarn or a stitch holder. Place both pocket flaps aside until needed.

Body

The body begins with the same ribbing as the sleeves. The body is worked flat in one piece from the hem to the underarms, then the fronts and back are worked separately to the shoulders. Pockets are knit in, and the button and buttonhole bands are worked at the front edges. Since this garment has unisex shaping, you can choose to work buttonholes on either side of the cardigan.

CO 211 (227, 247, 263, 283, 299, 319, 335, 355) sts. PM after first 11 and before last 11 sts to mark the button and buttonhole bands respectively. Work in K1, P1 ribbing for 3", working first buttonhole at 1.5" above cast-on edge.

Setup Row (RS): (K1, P1) 5 times, SSK removing marker, PM, work from Fiddlehead (right) chart over next 39 sts, work from Diamond Brocade chart over the next 8 (12, 17, 21, 26, 30, 35, 39, 44) sts, PM to mark right underarm, continue working from Diamond Brocade chart over the next 10 (14, 19, 23, 28, 32, 37, 41,

37, 41, 46) sts, work from Fiddlehead (left) and Fiddlehead (right) charts over the next 74 sts, omitting the first and last st of each chart, work from Diamond Brocade chart over the next 10 (14, 19, 23, 28, 32, 37, 41, 46) sts, PM to mark left underarm, continue working from Diamond Brocade chart over the next 8 (12, 17, 21, 26, 30, 35, 39, 44) sts, work from Fiddlehead (left) chart over next 39 sts, SM, work in rib to end. 210 (226, 246, 262, 282, 298, 318, 334, 354) sts. Continue working body, following charts as established.

AT THE SAME TIME, work buttonholes every 2.5" – to the neckline decreases.

AT THE SAME TIME, after working 31 (31, 35, 35, 38, 38, 42, 45, 45) rows in pattern, knit in the pockets.

Pocket Join Row (WS): Work across button band, SM, work in pattern for 19 (19, 20, 22, 24, 26, 27, 27, 29) sts. *Slip the live sts of one pocket on a spare needle. Holding the pocket in front of the work with the WS of both layers facing, purl the next stitch of the body together with the first stitch of the pocket. Place the next 20 (20, 23, 23, 25, 25, 27, 30, 30) sts of the body on a stitch holder or scrap yarn. Work across the pocket in pattern for the row of the body you are on, to the last st; purl this together with the next live stitch of the body. *

Work in pattern to 6 (10, 11, 13, 14, 16, 18, 19, 22) sts past the right underarm marker, and repeat between *s to attach the second pocket. Work in pattern to end of row.

Continue working Body from charts until piece measures 16 (16.5, 16.5, 16.5, 16.5, 15.5, 16.5, 16, 15.75)" from cast on.

Armholes

On the next RS row, stitches are bound off at each armhole. After this, the Fronts and Back are worked flat separately to the shoulders. Armhole and Neckline shaping occur AT THE SAME TIME, so read both sections before proceeding. The Neckline decreases will begin 4 (4, 5, 5, 5, 5, 7, 9, 11) rows after the armhole bind off. The final buttonhole is placed near the beginning of the Neckline decreases.

Next Row (RS): *Work to 1 (2, 2, 4, 5, 5, 6, 9, 9) sts before the right underarm marker. BO the next 2 (4, 4, 8, 10, 10, 12, 18, 18) sts, removing marker. Repeat from * at left underarm marker. 92 (98, 108, 112, 120, 128, 136, 138, 148) sts across Back, 47 (51, 56, 60, 65, 69, 74, 78, 83) sts across Right /Left Front excluding 11-st Button Band

Place Back sts on scrap yarn or a stitch holder, and work flat across Front sts only.
Work one (WS) row plain, attaching a new ball of yarn at the armhole side of the Right Front, and working Left and Right Fronts together. Neckline decreases are worked at the same time as armhole decreases.

Armhole Double Decrease Row:

RS: Work across Right Front in pattern to last 3 sts, SSSK. K3tog, work across Left front in pattern..
WS: Work across Left Front in pattern to last 3 sts, P3tog. P3tog TBL, work across Right Front in pattern.

Armhole Single Decrease Row:

RS: Work across Right Front in pattern to last 2 sts, SSK. K2tog, work across Left Front in pattern.
WS: Work across Left Front in pattern to last 2 sts, P2tog. P2tog TBL, work across Right Front in pattern.

Starting at the Right Front Button Band and working both Left Front and Right Front together:
Work Double Decrease row 0 (0, 0, 0, 0, 1, 3, 3, 3) times.
Work Single Decrease row 2 (2, 2, 3, 5, 6, 4, 5, 8) times.
Work Single Decrease row every other row 1 (1, 3, 3, 4, 4, 6, 6, 6) times.
Work Single Decrease row every third row 2 (1, 2, 2, 2, 2, 1, 1, 1) times.
(Work 6 (4, 3, 4, 3, 3, 3, 3, 5) rows even and then Single Decrease row) 1 (2, 1, 1, 1, 1, 1, 1, 1) times.

AT THE SAME TIME, place last buttonhole and work Neckline decreases.

Neckline

The neckline is bound off into the Fiddlehead pattern on the fronts of the cardigan. As you remove stitches, only complete the cables in the pattern that have enough stitches to work. When there are not enough stitches to complete a cable, work these remaining stitches in St st.

Neckline Decrease Row:

RS: Work to last st of Right Button Band, SSK with next Body stitch, work across Right Front in pattern to end. Work in pattern across Left Front to 2 sts before Button Band, K2tog, work across Left Button Band.
WS: Work to last st of Left Button Band, P2tog with next Body stitch, work across Left Front in pattern to end. Work in pattern across Right Front to last 2 sts before Button Band, P2tog TBL, work across Right Button Band.

Shape Neckline:

Work first Neckline Decrease Row on the 4th (1st, 1st, 1st, 1st, 1st, 4th, 6th)(row after the armhole bind off, then every 3rd row 16 (19, 20, 21, 22, 23, 23, 23, 23) times.

Work 6 (1, 3, 2, 1, 0, 0, 0, 0) rows with no shaping. 23 (23, 25, 25, 25, 26, 26, 26, 28) sts remain on each shoulder, not counting Button Band sts.

Short Rows

A set of short rows finishes off the shoulders. Work each shoulder separately.

Right Shoulder

Short Row 1 (RS): Work to 5 (6, 6, 7, 7, 7, 8, 8, 8) sts before the end, W&T.
Short Row 2 (WS): Work in pattern to end of row.
Short Row 3: Work to 5 (6, 6, 7, 7, 7, 8, 8, 8) sts before the wrapped st, W&T.
Short Row 4: Work in pattern to end of row.

Next Row: Turn and work across all sts, picking up wrapped sts and knitting them together with the sts they wrap.

Break yarn and put shoulder on st holder or scrap yarn.

Left Shoulder

Short Row 1 (RS): Work in pattern to end of row.
Short Row 2 (WS): Work to 5 (6, 6, 7, 7, 7, 8, 8, 8) sts before the end, W&T.
Short Row 3: Work in pattern to end of row.
Short Row 4: Work to 5 (6, 6, 7, 7, 7, 8, 8, 8) sts before the wrapped st, W&T.

Next Row: Turn and work across all sts, picking up wrapped sts and knitting them together with the sts they wrap.

Break yarn and put shoulder on st holder or scrap yarn.

Back

Place 92 (98, 108, 112, 120, 128, 136, 138, 148) held Back sts back on needles, and attach yarn ready to begin a WS row. Work 1 row in pattern.

Armhole Double Decrease Row

RS: K3tog, work in pattern to last 3 sts, SSSK.
WS: P3tog TBL, work in pattern to last 3 sts, P3tog.

Armhole Single Decrease Row

RS: K2tog, work in pattern to last 2 sts, SSK.
WS: P2tog TBL, work in pattern to last 2 sts, P2tog.

Work through Armhole shaping directions as for Front. 80 (86, 92, 94, 96, 98, 100, 100, 104) sts remain.

Work 36 (36, 38, 39, 39, 40, 39, 41, 38) rows even in pattern so that the Back is almost (2 rows less than) the length as the Front just before the Shoulder Short Rows.
On the next RS row, sts are bound off at the back neck to form the neckline:
Next Row (RS): Work in pattern for 24 (24, 26, 26, 26, 26, 27, 27, 29) sts, BO the next 32 (38, 40, 42, 44, 46, 46, 46, 46) sts, then work in pattern to the end of row.

Turn and work in pattern to 2 sts before neckline edge of left shoulder; P2tog. Attach a new ball of yarn at the right shoulder; P2tog TBL across the first 2 sts, then P to end. 23 (23, 25, 25, 25, 26, 26, 26, 28) sts remain on each shoulder.

Short rows

Short Row 1 (RS): Work to 5 (6, 6, 7, 7, 7, 8, 8, 8) sts before the end, W&T.
Short Row 2 (WS): Work to 5 (6, 6, 7, 7, 7, 8, 8, 8) sts before the end, W&T.
Short Row 3: Work to 5 (6, 6, 7, 7, 7, 8, 8, 8) sts before the wrapped st, W&T.
Short Row 4: Work to 5 (6, 6, 7, 7, 7, 8, 8, 8) sts before the wrapped st, W&T.

Next Row: Turn and work across all sts, picking up wrapped sts and knitting them together with the sts they wrap.

Do not break yarn.

Join Shoulders

Turn body inside out.. Using the the 3-needle Bind-Off technique, join the 23 (23, 25, 25, 25, 26, 26, 26, 28) held sts of each Front shoulder with the corresponding Back sts. Leave the 11 sts of the Button and Buttonhole Bands on holders.

Finishing

Set in Sleeves

With right sides facing out, set sleeves into armhole openings, making sure that the center of each sleeve cap is placed at the shoulder seam and that the seam under the sleeve and bound off sts of the armhole are centered. Pin in place. Using yarn needle and yarn, begin at the underarm and sew sleeves into the armholes, using mattress stitch.

Pocket finishing

Turn the cardigan to the wrong side and lay on a flat surface. Whipstitch the three raw edges of each pocket to the WS of the body, making sure to keep the edges straight. Turn to the RS. Place the 20 (20, 23, 23, 25, 25, 27, 30, 30) held sts from the body onto the needles. Attach yarn, leaving a 12" tail and ready to begin a RS row.

Setup Row: (K1, P1) to last 2 (2, 1, 1, 1, 1, 1, 2, 2) sts. Kfb 1 (1, 0, 0, 0, 0, 0, 1, 1) times, K1.
Row 2: (P1, K1) to last st, P1.
Row 3: (K1, P1) to last st, K1.

Repeat Rows 2-3 three more times, then Row 2 once more.
BO all sts in rib. Break yarn, leaving a 12" tail.

Using the cast on and bind off tails, whipstitch the side edges of the ribbing to the body of the sweater.

Collar Extension

The collar is extended from the Button and Buttonhole Bands around the back neck.

Place the 11 sts of the Band on the needles. Attach yarn, ready to begin a RS row at the Right Front shoulder.

Setup Row (RS): (K1, P1) to last st, KFB. 12 sts; this extra stitch will become the selvedge used for attaching the collar to the back neck.

Work in K1, P1 rib for 5.5 (6, 6.5, 6.75, 7, 7.5, 7.5, 7.5, 7.5, 7.5)", ending with an RS row.

Final Row (WS): (P1, K1) to last 2 sts, P2tog. 11 sts.

Break yarn, leaving a long tail for grafting.

Place the 11 sts of the Band on a spare needle. Using the long yarn tail, graft the two live ends together.

Lay the collar across the back neck. Whipstitch the collar to the back along the selvedge st.

Sew buttons opposite buttonholes. Weave in ends. Wash and block to measurements.

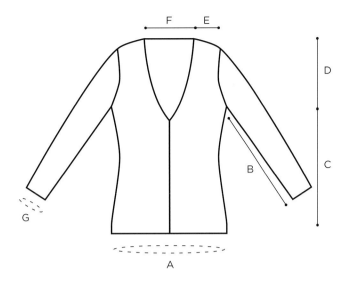

A 32 (36, 40, 44, 48, 52, 56, 60, 64)"
B 18.5 (18.5, 19.25, 20.25, 20.25, 20.25, 20, 19.25, 17.5, 16.5)"
C 16 (16.5, 16.5, 16.5, 15.5, 16.5, 16, 15.75)"
D 8.5 (8.5, 9, 9.5, 10, 10.5, 10.5, 10.75, 11.25)"
E 3.75 (3.75, 4, 4, 4, 4, 4.25, 4.25, 4.5)"
F 5.5 (6, 6.5, 6.75, 7, 7.5, 7.5, 7.5, 7.5)"
G 9 (9, 9.5, 10.25, 10.5, 11.5, 12, 12, 12)"

Fiddlehead (Right)

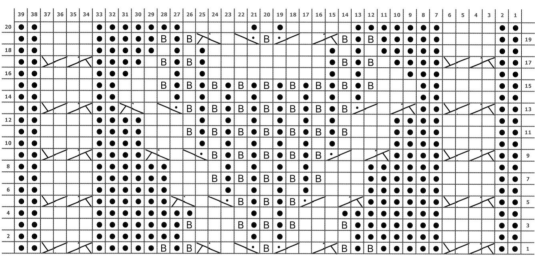

Fiddlehead (Left)

Legend

⦿	**purl**	RS: purl stitch WS: knit stitch
(c2 over 2 left symbol)	**c2 over 2 left**	RS: sl 2 to CN, hold in front. k2, k2 from CN WS: none defined
B	**knit tbl**	RS: Knit stitch through back loop WS: Purl stitch through back loop
(c3 over 2 right P symbol)	**c3 over 2 right P**	RS: sl2 to CN, hold in back. k3, then p2 from CN WS: none defined
(c3 over 2 left P symbol)	**c3 over 2 left P**	RS: sl3 to CN, hold in front. p2, then k3 from CN WS: none defined
□	**knit**	RS: knit stitch WS: purl stitch
□	**Pattern Repeat**	

Diamond Brocade

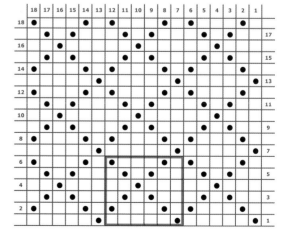

Sleeve

Begin reading the chart from the line indicating your size around the sleeve. As you increase, work the new stitches in the Diamond Brocade pattern. Note that the Diamond Brocade pattern has a 6-row repeat and the Fiddlehead pattern has a 20-row repeat.

PRINCESS PULLOVER

by Kerin Dimeler-Laurence

FINISHED MEASUREMENTS
32 (36, 40, 44, 48, 52, 56, 60, 64)" finished bust measurement

YARN
Knit Picks Galileo (50% Merino Wool, 50% Viscose from Bamboo; 131 yards/50g): Gem 26104, 13 (13, 14, 15, 16, 17, 18, 19, 20) balls.

NEEDLES
US 3 (3.25mm) DPNs and 24-48" circular needles, or long circulars for Magic Loop, or size to obtain gauge
US 2 (2.75mm) DPNs and 24-48" circular needles, or long circular needles for Magic Loop, or one size smaller than those used to obtain gauge

NOTIONS
Tapestry Needle
Stitch markers
Scrap yarn or stitch holders
Crochet hook for provisional CO
Scrap yarn for provisional CO

GAUGE
31 sts and 38 rows = 4" over Cable pattern in the round, blocked.
24 sts and 38 rows = 4" in St st in the round, blocked.

Princess Pullover

Notes:

With its flattering princess shaping and traditional stitch patterns, this pullover is a feminine, modern version of a classic Aran sweater. All references to *Right* and *Left* are as worn, unless otherwise noted.

Provisional Cast On (Crochet Chain method)

Using a crochet hook several sizes too big for the yarn, make a slipknot and chain for 1". Hold knitting needle in left hand. With yarn in back of the needle, work next chain st by pulling the yarn over the needle and through the chain st. Move yarn under and behind needle, and repeat for the number of sts required. Chain a few more sts off the needle, then break yarn and pull end through last chain. CO sts will be incorrectly mounted; knit into the back of these sts. To unravel (when sts need to be picked up), pull chain end out, and the chain should unravel, leaving live sts.

Join hem

Unravel provisional CO and place sts on spare needle. Hold these sts in back of the working needle, and work across row in pattern, working one st from front needle and one from the back k-wise together as one. This is worked like a Three-Needle Bind Off, without binding off.

M1L (Make 1 Left-leaning stitch): PU the bar between st just worked and next st and place on LH needle mounted as a regular knit stitch; knit through the back of the loop.

M1R (Make 1 Right-leaning stitch): PU the bar between st just worked and next st and place on LH needle backwards (incorrect stitch mount). Knit through the front of the loop.

Three-needle Bind Off

Hold the two pieces of knitting together with the points of the needles facing to the right. Insert a third needle into the first stitch on each of the needles knitwise, starting with the front needle. Work a knit stitch, pulling the loop through both of the stitches you've inserted the third needle through. After you've pulled the loop through, slip the first stitch off of each of the needles. This takes two stitches (one from the front needle and one from the back) and joins them to make one finished stitch on the third needle (held in your right hand). Repeat this motion, inserting your needle into one stitch on the front and back needles, knitting them together and slipping them off of the needles. Each time you complete a second stitch, pass the first finished stitch over the second and off of the needle (as you would in a traditional bind-off).

DIRECTIONS
Sleeves (Make two)

The sleeves begin at the wrist and are increased to the underarm. Turned hems allow them to lay flat.

Provisionally CO 60 (60, 62, 64, 68, 74, 78, 80, 82) sts onto smaller needles. Attach working yarn, and knit across all sts. Join to work in the round, being careful not to twist sts. Knit 9 rounds, then purl one round (turning round). Switch to larger needles.

Set up pattern: K 7 (7, 8, 9, 11, 14, 16, 17, 18) sts, work from round 1 of Sleeve chart over the next 46 sts, K to end.

Continue working in pattern as established, with St st flanking the central 46-st motif, through the first 8 rounds. On the next round (the 9th round of the patterning), unravel Provisional CO and place sts on spare needles; work in pattern around the sleeve, joining the hem.

Sleeve Increases

From here, the sleeves are increased to the underarms. Work all increased sts in St st.

Increase Round: K1, M1L, work in pattern to last st, M1R, K1. 2 sts increased.

Continuing in pattern as established, work an Increase Round every 12th (10th, 9th, 8th, 6th, 5th, [4th and 9th], 4th, 4th) round 13 (16, 18, 20, 27, 28, 16, 36, 38)times. 86 (92, 98, 104, 120, 128, 142, 152, 158) sts on the needles.

Knit 5 (2, 1, 3, 15, 12, 9, 22, 6) rounds in pattern.

Sleeve Cap Shaping

The sleeve cap should begin on what will be a WS (odd-numbered on the chart) row; work an extra round if needed to be ready to work a WS row. On the next round, stitches are bound off at the base of the sleeve cap. The cap is then worked flat (back and forth) to the end.

Work to 4 (6, 6, 6, 7, 5, 4, 4, 3) sts before the end of the round. BO the last 4 (6, 6, 6, 7, 5, 4, 4, 3) sts of the round, then the first 6 (8, 8, 8, 9, 7, 6, 6, 5) sts of the next round. Work in pattern to the last 3 sts of the row, SSSK. You are now working flat over 78 (80, 86, 92, 106, 118, 134, 144, 152) sts.

Shape the caps as follows.

Double Decrease Row (2 sts decreased at each edge):
RS: K3tog , work in pattern to last 3 sts, SSSK.
WS: P3tog TBL, work in pattern to last 3 sts, P3tog.

Single Decrease Row (1 st decreased at each edge):
RS: K2tog , work in pattern to last 2 sts, SSK.
WS: P2tog TBL, work in pattern to last 2 sts, P3tog.

Work a Double Decrease Row every row 2 (2, 1, 1, 3, 3, 5, 2, 0) times; work a Single Decrease Row every row 4 (5, 6, 4, 5, 3, 7, 15, 16) times, then every other row 7 (3, 6, 5, 3, 7, 4, 2, 8) times, then every third row 3 (6, 5, 7, 4, 7, 7, 3, 4) times, then every other row 6 (2, 3, 3, 9, 9, 6, 12, 9) times, then every row 5 (2, 3, 6, 2, 3, 8, 7, 9) times; work a Double Decrease Row every row 1 (3, 3, 2, 3, 3, 3, 4, 4) times.

After the last row of the Sleeve Cap, BO remaining 16 (24, 24, 30, 36, 36, 38, 42, 44) sts.

Body

The body begins with the same turned hem as the sleeves. All of the waist shaping is worked in the Cable Panel.

Provisionally CO 264 (296, 320, 340, 372, 396, 420, 456, 484) sts onto smaller needles. Attach working yarn and knit across all sts. PM and join to work in the round, being careful not to twist sts. Knit 9 rounds, then purl one round (turning round). Switch to larger needles.

Set up pattern: *K 13 (14, 17, 21, 26, 26, 30, 39, 45) sts, work from first round for your size of Cable Panel chart over the next 106 (120, 126, 128, 134, 146, 150, 150, 152) sts, K 13 (14, 17, 21, 26, 26, 30, 39, 45)*, PM to mark right underarm, repeat between *s across back.

Continue working in pattern as established, with St st flanking the central cable panel, through the first 8 rounds for your size. On the next round (the 9th round of the patterning for your size), unravel Provisional CO and place sts on spare needles; work in pattern around the body, joining the hem.

Work as established, working St st up the sides of the Body and Cable Panels on front and back. Repeat rounds 153-160 of the Center Panel chart through the armhole, neck and back. At the round noted for your size, BO for armholes, then work repeats of the Center Panel, armhole and neckline decreases at the same time. 118 (234, 146, 156, 172, 184, 196, 214, 228) sts each on front and back; 236 (268, 292, 312, 344, 368, 392, 428, 456) sts overall.

Armholes

At the round in the Center Panel chart noted for your size, stitches are bound off at each armhole. After this, the Front and Back are worked flat separately to the shoulders.

Work to 2 (2, 2, 3, 3, 5, 7, 9, 11) sts before the right underarm marker. BO the next 4 (4, 4, 6, 6, 10, 14, 18, 22) sts, removing marker. Repeat at left underarm marker. 114 (130, 142, 150, 166, 174, 182, 196, 206) sts remain across both Front and Back.

Place Back sts on scrap yarn or a stitch holder, and work flat across Front sts only.

Front

Work one (RS) row plain.

Armhole Double Decrease Row:
RS: K3tog, K to last 3 sts, SSSK.
WS: P3tog TBL, P to last 3 sts, P3tog.

Armhole Single Decrease Row:
RS: K2tog, K to last 2 sts, SSK.
WS: P2tog TBL, P to last 2 sts, P2tog.

Work an Armhole Double Decrease Row every row 1 (1, 1, 2, 4, 2, 4, 7, 7) times; work an Armhole Single Decrease Row every row 4 (4, 5, 7, 6, 6, 7, 7, 11) times, then every other row 2 (3, 4, 3, 6, 5, 2, 5, 6) times, then every 3rd row 2 (0, 3, 3, 2, 3, 4, 2, 2) times; follow additional instructions for your size below.

Size 32": Work 6 rows in pattern, then work an Armhole Single Decrease Row. 92 sts remain across front.

Size 36": Work an Armhole Double Decrease Row every 4th row twice; work 7 rows in pattern, work an Armhole Single Decrease Row. 102 sts remain across front.

Size 40": Work 6 rows in pattern, work an Armhole Single Decrease Row. 112 sts remain across front.

Size 44": Work 6 rows in pattern, work an Armhole Single Decrease Row. 114 sts remain across front.

Size 48": Work 3 rows in pattern, work an Armhole Single

Decrease Row. 120 sts remain across front.

Size 52": Work 4 rows in pattern, work an Armhole Single Decrease Row, work 7 rows in pattern, work an Armhole Single Decrease Row. 134 sts remain across front.

Size 56": Work an Armhole Single Decrease Row every 5th row twice. 136 sts remain across front.

Size 60": Work an Armhole Double Decrease Row every 4th row twice. 136 sts remain across front.

Size 64": Work 5 rows in pattern, work an Armhole Single Decrease Row. 138 sts remain across front.

Work 15 (7, 13, 17, 22, 25, 26, 32, 33) rows in pattern.

Neckline

On the next RS row, sts are bound off at the front neck to form the neckline.

Knit 40 (41, 46, 47, 49, 54, 55, 55, 56) sts, BO the next 12 (20, 20, 20, 22, 26, 26, 26, 26) sts; K to end. Follow neckline decrease directions below; attach a second ball of yarn at the left neckline edge and work both sides of the neckline together.

Neckline Double Decrease Row:
RS: Work in pattern to last 3 sts of left neck edge, SSSK. K3tog, work in pattern across right shoulder.
WS: Work in pattern to last 3 sts of right neck edge, P3tog. P3tog TBL, work in pattern across left shoulder.

Neckline Decrease Row:
RS: Work in pattern to last 2 sts of left neck edge, SSK. K2tog, work in pattern across right shoulder.
WS: Work in pattern to last 2 sts of right neck edge, P2tog. P2tog TBL, work in pattern across left shoulder.

Shape Neckline:
Work a Neckline Double Decrease Row every row 4 (3, 2, 5, 2, 4, 3, 3, 3) times, then work a Neckline Single Decrease Row every row 2 (5, 5, 5, 6, 2, 4, 4, 5) times, then every other row 4 (3, 4, 3, 4, 4, 5, 6, 4) times, then every third row 2 (2, 2, 3, 3, 3, 2, 2, 3) times. 16 (16, 15, 17, 17, 17, 17, 18, 18) sts have been removed from each front; 24 (25, 31, 26, 32, 37, 38, 37, 38) sts remain on each shoulder.

Short rows
A set of short rows finishes off the shoulders.

Short Row 1 (RS): Work in pattern to to 7 (8, 9, 9, 10, 11, 11, 11, 12) sts before the end of the Right shoulder; W&T.
Short Row 2 (WS): Work in pattern to 7 (8, 9, 9, 10, 11, 11, 11, 12) sts before the end of the Left shoulder; W&T.
Short Row 3: Work in pattern to 7 (8, 9, 9, 10, 11, 11, 11, 12) sts before the last wrapped st, W&T.
Short Row 4: Work in pattern to 7 (8, 9, 9, 10, 11, 11, 11, 12) sts before the wrapped st, W&T.
Next Row (RS): Turn and knit across all sts, picking up wrapped sts and knitting them together with the sts they wrap.

Break yarn and put shoulders on st holders or scrap yarn.

Back

Place 114 (130, 142, 150, 166, 174, 182, 196, 206) Back sts back on needles, and attach yarn ready to begin a RS row. Work through Armhole shaping directions as for Front. 92 (102, 112, 114, 120, 134, 136, 136, 138) sts remain.

Work 47 (42, 47, 51, 57, 64, 68, 70, 73) rows in pattern.

On the next RS row, sts are bound off at the back neck to form the neckline.

Work in pattern for 25 (26, 32, 27, 33, 38, 39, 38, 39) sts, BO the next 42 (50, 48, 60, 54, 58, 58, 60, 60) sts, then work in pattern to the end of row.

Turn and work in pattern to 2 sts before neckline edge of left shoulder; P2tog. Attach a new ball of yarn at the right shoulder; P2tog TBL across the first 2 sts, then work in pattern to end. 24 (25, 31, 26, 32, 37, 38, 37, 38) sts remain on each shoulder.

Work short rows as for Front, working the Back left shoulder as for the Front right and the Back right as the Front left, Do not break yarn.

Join Shoulders

Turn body inside out, and join the shoulders together using working yarn from the back and the 3-needle Bind-Off technique.

Finishing

Set in Sleeves

With right sides facing out, set sleeves into armhole openings, making sure that the center of each sleeve cap is placed at the shoulder seam and that the seam under the sleeve and bound off sts of the armhole are centered. Pin in place. Using yarn needle and yarn, begin at the underarm and sew sleeves into the armholes, using mattress stitch.

Collar

The collar is worked as a rolled crew neck. Use smaller needles.

With RS facing and starting at right shoulder seam, PU and K 2 sts to the first bound off st at the back neck, 42 (50, 48, 60, 54, 58, 58, 60, 60) sts across the bound off sts at the back neck, 2 sts up to the left shoulder seam, and 42 (50, 48, 60, 54, 58, 58, 60, 60) around front neckline edge back to right shoulder. 88 (104, 100, 124, 112, 120, 120, 124, 124) sts. PM and join to work in the round.

Work in K2, P2 rib for 2". Break yarn, leaving a tail of several yards. Fold the collar towards the inside. Using the yarn tail, whipstitch the live sts to the back of the picked up row.

Weave in ends. Wash and block to measurements.

Sleeve

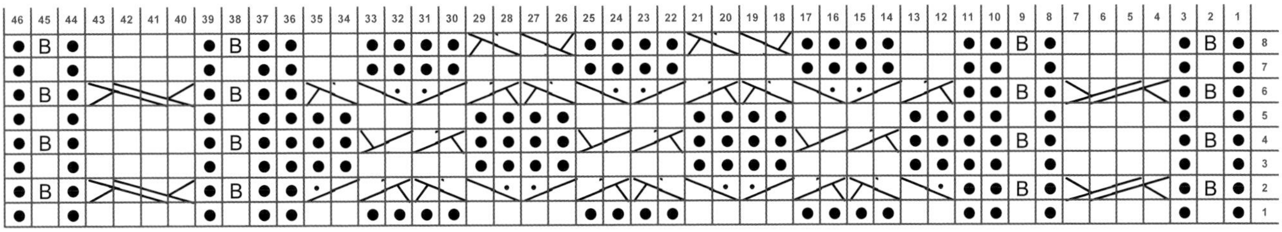

Legend

- ● **purl** — purl stitch
- □ **knit** — knit stitch
- B **knit tbl** — Knit stitch through back loop
- ⤫ **c2 over 2 right** — sl2 to CN, hold in back. k2, k2 from CN
- ⤫ **c1 over 3 right** — sl3 st to CN, hold in back. k1, k3 from CN
- ⤫ **c2 over 2 right P** — sl2 to CN, hold in back. k2, p2 from CN
- ⤫ **c2 over 2 left P** — sl 2 to CN, hold in front. p2, k2 from CN
- ⤫ **c1 over 3 left** — sl1 to CN, hold in front. k3, k1 from CN
- ⤫ **c2 over 2 left** — sl 2 to CN, hold in front. k2, k2 from CN
- ⤫ **c2 over 1 right P** — sl1 to CN, hold in back. k2, p1 from CN
- ⤫ **c2 over 1 left P** — sl2 to CN, hold in front. p1, k2 from CN
- ⁄ **p2tog** — Purl 2 stitches together
- ■ **No Stitch** — Placeholder - No stitch made.
- Φ **Purl Front and Back** — Purl into the front and back of the stitch; 1 stitch added.

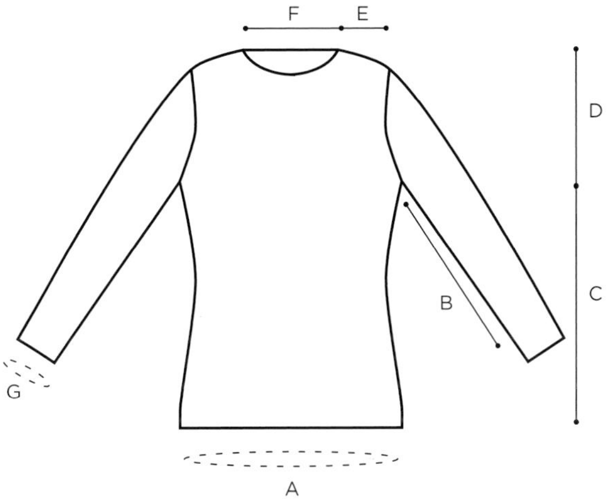

A 32 (36, 40, 44, 48, 52, 56, 60, 64)"
B 18 (18.25, 18.25, 18.25, 19, 16.5, 17, 18.5, 17.5)"
C 16.25 (15.75, 16.5, 16.5, 17.5, 16.25, 16.5, 16.5, 16.25)"
D 8 (8.25, 9, 9.5, 10.25, 11.75, 12, 12.5, 12.75)"
E 3 (3.25, 4, 3.25, 4.25, 4.75, 5, 4.75, 5)"
F 5.5 (6.5, 6.25, 7.75, 7, 7.5, 7.5, 7.75, 7.75)"
G 8.5 (8, 8.75, 9, 9.75, 10.5, 11.25, 11.5, 12)"

Cable Panel (part 1)

Work this st 3 (2, 1, 2, 1, 3, 1, 1, 2) times.

Work these 8 sts 4 (6, 7, 7, 8, 9, 10, 10, 10) times.

Work this st 3 (2, 1, 2, 1, 3, 1, 1, 2) times.

Cable Panel (part 2)

Work this st 3 (2, 1, 2, 1, 3, 1, 2) times.

Work these 8 sts 4 (6, 7, 7, 8, 9, 10, 10, 10) times.

Work this st 3 (2, 1, 2, 1, 3, 1, 2) times.

32"
36"
40"
44"
48"
52"
56"
60"
64"

Cable Panel (part 1)

Work this st 3 (2, 1, 2, 1, 3, 1, 1, 2) times.

Work these 8 sts 4 (6, 7, 7, 8, 9, 10, 10, 10) times.

Work this st 3 (2, 1, 2, 1, 3, 1, 1, 2) times.

Cable Panel (part 3)

Work through rows 153-160, then BO for armholes on the first round of the second repeat (round 161)

52, 56

60, 64

32, 36, 40, 48

Work two repeats of rows 153-160, then BO for armholes on the first round of the third repeat (round 169)

Work this st 3 (2, 1, 2, 1, 3, 1, 1, 2) times.

Work these 8 sts 4 (6, 7, 7, 8, 9, 10, 10, 10) times.

Work this st 3 (2, 1, 2, 1, 3, 1, 1, 2) times.

Work this st 3 (2, 1, 2, 1, 3, 1, 1, 2) times.

For pattern support, please contact customerservice@knitpicks.com

Abbreviations

BO	bind off	M	marker		stitch	TBL	through back loop
cn	cable needle	M1	make one stitch	RH	right hand	TFL	through front loop
CC	contrast color	M1L	make one left-leaning	rnd(s)	round(s)	tog	together
CDD	Centered double dec		stitch	RS	right side	W&T	wrap & turn (see
CO	cast on	M1R	make one right-lean-	Sk	skip		specific instructions
cont	continue		ing stitch	Sk2p	sl 1, k2tog, pass		in pattern)
dec	decrease(es)	MC	main color		slipped stitch over	WE	work even
DPN(s)	double pointed	P	purl		k2tog: 2 sts dec	WS	wrong side
	needle(s)	P2tog	purl 2 sts together	SKP	sl, k, psso: 1 st dec	WYIB	with yarn in back
EOR	every other row	PM	place marker	SL	slip	WYIF	with yarn in front
inc	increase	PFB	purl into the front and	SM	slip marker	YO	yarn over
K	knit		back of stitch	SSK	sl, sl, k these 2 sts tog		
K2tog	knit two sts together	PSSO	pass slipped stitch	SSP	sl, sl, p these 2 sts tog		
KFB	knit into the front and		over		tbl		
	back of stitch	PU	pick up	SSSK	sl, sl, sl, k these 3 sts		
K-wise	knitwise	P-wise	purlwise		tog		
LH	left hand	rep	repeat	St st	stockinette stitch		
		Rev St st	reverse stockinette	sts	stitch(es)		

Knit Picks yarn is both luxe and affordable—a seeming contradiction trounced! But it's not just about the pretty colors; we also care deeply about fiber quality and fair labor practices, leaving you with a gorgeously reliable product you'll turn to time and time again.

THIS COLLECTION FEATURES

Galileo
Sport Weight
50% Merino Wool, 50% Viscose from Bamboo

Wool of the Andes Tweed
Worsted Weight
80% Peruvian Highland Wool, 20% Donegal Tweed

Wool of the Andes
Worsted Weight
100% Peruvian Highland Wool

Wool of the Andes Superwash
Worsted Weight
100% Superwash Wool

Palette
Fingering Weight
100% Peruvian Highland Wool

View these beautiful yarns and more at www.KnitPicks.com